Peter Fritzsche

Hamsters

Everything About Selection, Care, Nutrition, and Behavior

Filled with Full-color Photographs by Oliver Giel

BARRON'S

50 Staying Active

Appendix

First Contact

Button eyes, a wiggly nose, and a comical nature. Golden Hamsters sure do look cute—but they are much more demanding than they appear at first glance. If you want to keep your hamster properly, you surely will want to find out as much as you can in advance.

Good Things Come in Small Packages!

Many children want to have their own pet. In the search for a playmate that's easy to care for, many stumble onto hamsters. It looks so simple: practically every pet shop has a supply of the comical little critters. So off you go to the nearest shop, where you buy a hamster complete with a cage. But wait! Aside from the responsibility you have to assume for an animal, hamsters have their own idiosyncrasies. And for precisely this reason, they are not among the least demanding pets. For children under the age of 12 they are not appropriate at all. Why? Here are just a couple of reasons: Hamsters live alone and don't like company. They don't like to be held, and they easily experience stress. They are active at night, so they want to sleep when we are awake. And their life expectancy is quite short at around two years. Are you sure you can deal with all this—and after reading this handbook are you still (or newly) interested in owning a hamster? Then you will have lots of pleasure with your new houseguest. I wrote this book so that things would go well in your lives together.

The Variety of Types

Before buying a hamster, you need to decide what kind you want. There are about 20 different types of hamsters (experts are not in agreement about the precise number). But only five of them are appropriate as pets: Golden Hamsters, Djungarian Dwarf Hamsters, Campbell's Dwarf Hamsters, Roborovskii's Dwarf Hamsters, and Chinese Hamsters. You will find more about their characteristics starting on page 12.

The Golden Hamster Story

Even though nearly every child today knows what a Golden Hamster looks like, not too long ago these animals were totally unknown to us. In many places the hamster has been known only since the 1940s, so it has been a house pet for only a relatively short time.

How It All Began

In 1797 the Golden Hamster was mentioned in literature for the first time. In 1839 it was described scientifically and given its name: *Mesocricetus auratus*. The first word (*Mesocricetus*) is the genus name, and it means "medium hamster." In addition to the Golden Hamster, this genus includes three other species. *Auratus* is the species name, and it means *golden*.

But it took almost another hundred years before a living hamster was found. In 1930 the Israeli zoologist Israel Aharoni dug up a mother hamster

To escape discovery by an enemy animal, this wild hamster presses flat against the ground as it carefully creeps to the nearest food plant.

with eleven young in a wheat field in Syria, of which one female and three males survived. To this day, all pet hamsters in the world are descended from the mating of these four hamsters.

Expeditions into Hamster Country

Since the small animals can be bred quickly and successfully, not much research was done on them in their homeland. Only since the behavior of Golden Hamsters was studied scientifically at the Institute for Zoology in Halle, Germany, starting in 1975, after many discoveries in the laboratory there arose a desire to observe the animals in the wild. In 1999 we traveled on an expedition to Syria under the direction of Professor Rolf Gattermann. The digging was successful: 19 wild hamsters came back to Halle with us. I still remember the great joy of seeing the first Golden Hamsters in the wild.

Dwarf Hamsters

Even more recent than the history of the Golden Hamster is that of its smaller "relatives," the Dwarf Hamsters. They have been sold in shops and kept as pets only since the 1980s. The history of the Djungarian Dwarf Hamster can be followed back the farthest. It was discovered and described as early as 1773 by the German Simon Pallas on one of his distant travels. The other three species presented in this book—Campbell's Dwarf Hamsters, Roborovskii's Dwarf Hamsters, and Chinese Striped Hamsters—were described scientifically shortly before or after the start of the 20th century. During this time many research expeditions into their natural habitats have been undertaken.

The Right Pet for You

TIPS FROM
THE HAMSTER PRO
Peter Fritzsche

A hamster is the right animal for you only if all of the following statements apply to you:

DISTANCE: I would like an animal I can watch, not cuddle.

SOLITARY CREATURE: I can deal with the fact that my hamster is a loner, active at night, and at rest during the day.

AGE: I know that my hamster will live to be only about two years old.

ACTIVITY: I can provide my pet with a large cage and a variety of accessories, plus opportunities to run around safely inside the house.

RESPECT: I know that hamsters don't like being held in my hand.

GOOD CARE: I know someone who can take care of my hamster if I go away.

RESPONSIBILITY: I am older than 12 and ready to take care of my hamster every day.

Where Do Hamsters Live?

There are wild hamsters in all of Europe and Asia. The field hamster, the largest species, even lives in northern European countries such as Germany. But all the species that are suited to keeping as pets come from Asia. The wild Golden Hamster, for example, comes only from the north of Syria and a narrow strip of land in southern Turkey. As a result, the species has a very limited range and is correspondingly under serious threat. In order to observe Campbell's Dwarf Hamsters, Djungarian Dwarf Hamsters, Roborovskii's Dwarf Hamsters, or Chinese Hamsters in the wild, you have to travel farther still: in eastern Russia, beyond Kazakhstan, in Mongolia, and beyond China. There they live primarily in the steppes and semi-desert areas with scant vegetation. Roborovskii's Dwarf Hamsters have even adapted to the hard conditions of the Mongolian and Chinese deserts. Golden Hamsters, on the other hand, prefer managed fields to the meager floors of the steppes and deserts. Lentil fields in particular appeal to the little rodents. It's really an experience to watch them in the evening hours as they assiduously hoard plants. It's no wonder that they are not welcome guests with farmers, who even use chemical agents to combat them. And when I told a Syrian farmer that in Europe Golden Hamsters are kept as pets, he merely laughed in disbelief.

How Do Hamsters Live?

The first thing about the hamster's lifestyle is that they live all alone. Golden Hamsters in particular react negatively when they meet others of their kind. They avoid one another or get into real fights. Of course, one exception is the mating season, in which the males actively search for female Golden Hamsters. But after mating, they once again leave the female, if they don't want to be driven away. Dwarf Hamsters are not as insistent on being alone.

When a hamster is certain that no danger threatens, it leaves its burrow in search of food.

The males even help a little in raising the young. But to date not much has been known about the life of the Dwarf Hamster in the wild—field research is in its infancy. But people who own Dwarf Hamsters know that their pets can tolerate one another even in pairs (also see p.17).

In the wild, all hamsters live most of the time during the day in underground burrows that they dig themselves. They feel safe there, so they disappear into the underground passageways at the slightest disturbance. The burrows go down as far as three feet (1 m) into the earth and generally have just one entrance and exit. These vertical tunnels make it easy to distinguish hamster burrows from those of other small mammals (e.g.,

mice). Formerly, scientists believed that hamsters were active outside the burrow throughout the night. But today we know that Golden Hamsters leave their burrow about an hour before sundown. When it gets dark, they disappear into it once again, before reappearing the following morning for about an hour to search for food.

Hibernation Winters in the Golden Hamster's original habitat can be very hard. The animals therefore lower their body temperature, roll up into a ball, and hibernate. Dwarf hamsters cannot do this.

Do You Know Hamsters?

DID YOU KNOW THAT ...	AND THAT...
... hamsters generally live alone?	... they wake up about every five days to eat?
... hamsters spend 90% of their life in their burrow?	... Djungarian Hamsters fall into winter torpor?
... in the winter and during major drought, hamsters block up their burrow with earth?	... at low temperatures in the winter, Djungarian Dwarf Hamsters develop a white coat?
... Field Hamsters can hoard up to 110 lbs. of food?	... Dwarf Hamsters do not hibernate?
... a Golden Hamster's heart beats about four and a half times faster than that of a human?	... in the spring, Golden Hamsters spend 20 hours a day inside their burrows?
... hamsters see poorly and are nearly color blind?	... Golden Hamsters stay in during drought?
... hamsters hear well and have an even stronger sense of smell?	... female hamsters are ready to mate every fourth night in the spring?
... hamsters can also produce ultrasonic sounds?	... a change of cage is very stressful for hamsters?
... when days grow shorter and temperatures dip below 46°F (8° C), hamsters hibernate?	... with males, the testes protrude from the stomach to keep the sperm cool?

Hamster Facts

Ears

Hamsters can hear very well. They are particularly capable of perceiving high pitches—even in the realm of ultrasound. So avoid all squeaking noises and shrill sounds to keep from frightening these sensitive creatures.

Paws

The front paws have four toes. Hamsters use them to hold their food and to groom themselves. The animals are capable of standing erect on the larger hind paws with their five toes. An important point for well-being: the claws must have an opportunity to get worn down, preferably on wood.

Sex

With young animals it is not always easy to distinguish between the sexes. One characteristic is the distance between the anus and the opening for the sex organ; with females (left) it is smaller than with males (right). In addition, it is almost always possible to identify the testicles in a male.

Eyes

Hamsters cannot see very well with their cute button eyes. They are nearsighted and color-blind; they see shades of green and yellow the best–that's good for hoarding.

Teeth

The sharp incisors are a clear sign that hamsters are rodents. The four incisors grow continuously, so hamsters must always be able to wear them down. Food is ground up using the 12 molars.

Nose

Hamsters can smell very well. They can even recognize one another by scent and sometimes use their sense of smell to locate their partner. The hamster's whiskers are used to detect the edge of a precipice or the size of an opening.

Cheeks

The bulges in the mucous membrane of the mouth reach nearly back to the hind legs. A Golden Hamster can fill its cheek pouches with up to 3/4 oz. (20 g) of grain. They are emptied by repeatedly stroking them with the front legs.

An Overview of Hamster Types

The Golden Hamster is the type of hamster most commonly kept as a pet—but Dwarf Hamsters, too, are increasingly popular as pets.

Golden Hamsters

The wild form of the Golden Hamster (*Mesocricetus auratus*) has brown fur, a gray to white belly, and a dark cheek stripe. There are also breeding forms, however. The creatures grow up to seven inches (18 cm) long and weigh as much as 6 1/2 ounces (180 g). They are generally peaceable and they easily get used to people.

Dwarf Hamsters

Dwarf hamsters are scientifically known as short-tailed hamsters. However, this name has not gained acceptance among pet owners.

Campbell's Dwarf Hamsters and Djungarian Dwarf Hamsters (*Phodopus campbelli* and *Phodopus sungorus*) Because of their gray fur, whitish stomach, and black dorsal stripe, these two species are often mistaken for one another. But with the Djungarian Dwarf Hamster the contrast between belly and back coloration is much more clearly recognizable—this is a good distinguishing feature. With this species, the border between the upper and lower sides (the so-called three-curve line) is much clearer. Both species are about four inches (10 cm) long and weigh up to 1 3/4 oz. (50 g). As with the Golden Hamster, there are various breeding forms.

Roborovskii Dwarf Hamsters (*Phodopus roborovskii*) These mostly light brown to yellowish animals have no black dorsal stripe and are smaller than the two species previously mentioned. "Robos" are only 3 1/2 inches (9 cm) long and weigh only a little more than three-quarters of an ounce (25 g).

Chinese Hamsters (*Cricetulus griseus*) This species is colored like the Campbell's and Djungarian Dwarf Hamsters, but are noticeably longer and slightly larger than the others. The most reliable distinguishing feature is the long tail, which is longer than the rear foot.

Wild colored Golden Hamsters are relatively easy to care for, and quickly grow accustomed to people.

DJUNGARIAN DWARF HAMSTER The Djungarian is similar to the Campbell's Dwarf Hamster. Of all dwarf hamsters, this type adapts best to humans.

CAMPBELL'S DWARF HAMSTER With proper handling, this type adjusts well to humans and certainly is not as prone to biting as people commonly say.

CHINESE HAMSTER These animals are slimmer and have a longer tail than the other species. They need an experienced caregiver. This type can climb particularly well and is a good choice for hamster aficionados who have some experience.

ROBOROVSKII DWARF HAMSTERS The smallest dwarf hamster is also known as the desert hamster. These animals are as active as they are demanding, so they are not as well suited to children and beginning hamster owners.

Portraits of Hamster Breeds

In addition to the wild varieties, there are various breeding forms with special colors, checkered fur, or impressively long hair. But for beginners with hamsters, the easier-to-care-for wild forms are often a better choice.

CHECKERED HAMSTERS
Three-colored checkered hamsters are considered more aggressive and don't adapt easily to humans.

SOOT HAMSTERS Hamsters with pure white fur, and ones with black roots and dark ears are called Soot Hamsters. The breeding form is relatively friendly and easy to care for.

CHECKERED DJUNGARIAN
There are one- or multi-colored breeding forms not only with Golden, but also with dwarf hamsters. This Djungarian Dwarf Hamster has a white belly and a gray checkered back.

SATIN HAMSTERS This special breeding form with shiny, silky fur is hard to breed. This one is a gold- and copper-colored example.

LONGHAIRED HAMSTERS The so-called Teddy Hamsters are pleasant and peaceable, but their hair requires lots of care. A special breeding form is the Angora Hamster.

BLACK GOLDEN HAMSTER Single-colored breeding forms, such as this black animal, behave essentially the same as their wild colored relatives.

CHECKERED HAMSTER The two-colored checkered variant comes in a broad array of colors. This hamster has white fur with sprinklings of black. Other breeds are white and brown or gray and black.

SATIN HAMSTERS The cream-colored breeding form is similar to the Teddy Hamster in its peaceful disposition, and it adjusts relatively easily to people. Therefore, it is a good choice for beginners.

Home at Last

Will it be a Golden Hamster or a Dwarf Hamster? What do you need to be aware of in buying a Hamster and getting it home? What's the best type of cage, and how should it be set up to meet the requirements of your new pet most effectively? You will now find the answers to all these questions.

Which Hamster Is Best for Me?

The various types and breeds of hamsters are different not only in size and fur color—they also have different dispositions and behavior. Find the right animal for you.

A Golden Hamster ...

A wild colored Golden Hamster is the best housemate for (younger) children. This hamster, the largest variety kept as a pet, is easy to tame. Also, the single-color breeding forms such as pure white Golden Hamsters, are considered easy to care for. Checkered animals, on the other hand, are problematic, for they often are harder to tame. Longhaired Golden Hamsters, often available under the designation of "Teddy Hamsters," have a gentle nature like the wild colored animals. Since the long fur tangles easily, though, these animals require quite a lot of care.

Note: An important consideration no matter which form you choose: Golden Hamsters must be kept singly.

... or a Dwarf Hamster?

Among the "dwarfs," the Campbell's and Djungarian Dwarf Hamsters adapt most successfully to humans. Roborovskii's Dwarf Hamsters and Chinese Hamsters, on the other hand, are suitable only for watching. The recommendation to keep the animals singly also applies in principle to dwarfs. Still, these animals can sometimes be kept in pairs or small groups of the same sex. This is possible especially when the animals have grown up together. But even in this case, you should have a second cage ready so you can immediately separate any possible adversaries. My recommendation: it's best to keep even dwarf hamsters singly.

Getting the Cage Ready

To help your new pet settle in quickly, get everything ready at home before you make your purchase. The cage is the most important part.

The Right Location

First, think about where the cage should be placed. Consider your future charge's habit of resting during the day—so a place in the center of the living room or a child's bedroom is not a particularly good choice. The ideal spot is a room that gets little use during the day, or a quiet corner. In addition to disliking a constant stream of noise from television or radio, hamsters don't like bright light or sunshine, so a location near a window is out. Also think about placing the cage at eye level so that it's easier to watch your hamster.

Some Like It Cool As for room temperature, hamsters are not so demanding. In the winter, the cage can even be placed in an unheated room, but the temperature should not go below 59° F (15° C). Excessively high temperatures are even more uncomfortable, so make sure that the temperature in the cage doesn't exceed 77° F (25° C). In the hot summer months, you can cool the cage by placing moistened dishtowels over it.

Size and Type of Cage

In choosing a place for the cage, you also have to consider its size—the larger the better. A Golden Hamster's housing should be at least 32 inches long and 16 inches wide (80 × 40 cm). Dwarf hamsters can be kept in cages 24 inches (60 cm) long, but only if they are at least 16 inches (40 cm) wide. You shouldn't skimp on height. On the contrary: a lack of floor space can be alleviated considerably by the addition of several stories. With no intervening stories, the minimum height is 16 inches (40 cm). If you already have a smaller cage, it's a good idea to buy a second cage and connect the two through a short plastic tunnel. Many times hamsters are kept in retired aquariums.

Here's something to investigate: two Djungarian Dwarf Hamsters are putting their wooden cage accessories to the test.

These "cages" are not only more difficult to clean, but the air circulation is also greatly reduced. Thus the length of an aquarium should be at least three feet (1 m).

Homemade Many handy people build their own hamster cage. Wood construction with a front panel of acrylic glass is best. An appropriate cage lid and a mesh window provide ventilation from the side. As long as the minimum dimensions mentioned previously are observed, there are no limits to your imagination in equipping the cage—but use only untreated wood and solvent-free varnish.

Cage Bars The best material is galvanized steel wire. If the mesh is coated in some color or with plastic, the wire inside will soon be exposed through gnawing and will quickly begin to rust. With Golden Hamsters, the spaces in the wire mesh should be no larger than 1/2 inch (12 mm), and 5/16 inch (7 mm) with dwarf hamsters. Also, if the bars are arranged vertically, it's easier for the hamsters to climb on them than with horizontal ones.

Cage Floor A plastic tray, which can be easily removed for cleaning (preferably at the front), forms the bottom of the cage. The sides of the tray should be about four inches (10 cm) high to keep the bedding from falling out. As a ground dweller, the hamster will try to dig and make holes in the bedding. If the tray is too shallow, you can also attach some narrow plastic strips around the cage.

1 HOMEMADE An individually crafted wood masterpiece like this one is ideal for the hamster's needs.

2 ANOTHER STORY If the cage is large enough, it's a good idea to build on another story. That way you create more area for things to keep the hamster occupied.

3 TWIN PACK When two smaller cages are connected by a tunnel, they come very close to the conditions in a natural burrow.

Bedding

The bedding for the cage must be absorbent and free of dust and harmful substances. Good old wood chips are the best. They are sold in pet shops as small animal bedding. In order to create a natural appearance, the wood chips can be mixed with bark mulch. You should not use sawdust, peat moss, or kitty litter—and the special scented hamster bedding promoted in ads is not a good choice. The bedding should be an inch or two (3-5 cm) deep. If you have one dwarf hamster, it's also a good idea to put in a shallow bowl with fine chinchilla sand. The animals use it in their grooming.
Note: In pet shops, you can get special corner inserts made of plastic to place under the litter in the cage in the preferred toilet corner. For cleaning, you can simply lift the piece out of the cage and clean it separately.

Hamster Houses

The house inside the cage should be a substitute for the hamster's underground burrow and provide a place of retreat. Often hoarded food is also placed inside it, so the house should not be too small. And yet it must also provide for the animal's need for wall contact. For a Golden Hamster, a floor area of about four by eight inches (20 × 10 cm) is the right size. Of course, it can be a little smaller for dwarf hamsters. The structure should be closed on all sides and have a round entrance. For Golden Hamsters this opening is 1 3/4 inch (4.5 cm), and for dwarf hamsters it's about 1 1/2 inch (3.5 cm). It's best to have a flat roof so that the hamster can also use it for climbing. Ideally, the roof should be removable. That way, it's not necessary to move the whole house around if you have to check something, and the hamster won't have to set it up

again every time. For padding the hamster house, simply put some facial tissue or toilet paper into the cage. Never use what's known as hamster wool, for the animals can quickly get their feet tangled up in it.

Food and Water

Although most hamsters quickly hoard food in a corner of the cage or carry it into their house, you should not neglect to provide a food dish. This is the best place to offer fresh or live food. The dish should be made of porcelain or stoneware for stability. A diameter of 2 1/2 inches (6 cm) and a one-inch (2 cm) rim that curves inward are ideal. Dishes are not appropriate for water, however. Not only do they quickly become soiled, but many hamsters have also drowned in them. A hamster can drink at any time from a water bottle with an automatic double-ball valve hung on the outside of the cage.

Basic Accessories at a Glance

CAGE Sufficiently large, at least 16 x 32 inches (80 x 40 cm)
PLASTIC TRAY four inches (10 cm) deep
WOOD SHAVINGS for bedding
HAMSTER HOUSE about 4 x 8 inches (20 x 10 cm)
FOOD DISH stable, with a rim that curves inward, about 2 1/2 inches (6 cm) in diameter
WATER BOTTLE attached to the outside of the cage
SAND BATH for dwarf hamsters

EXERCISE WHEEL Although it is hotly debated among hamster owners, scientific research supports keeping an exercise wheel in the cage—as long as the running surface is continuous and the diameter is large enough so that the hamster doesn't injure itself or damage its spine. Make sure that the wheel is closed on one side and turns easily. You may need to lubricate it occasionally with a little cooking oil.

WATER BOTTLE Even if you regularly give your hamster fresh food, there should be a water bottle in the cage from which the animal can drink at will. Water bottles with a double-ball valve keep water from flowing out unnecessarily. But with these models, you also need to be sure that the valve doesn't get blocked by lime deposits from the water.

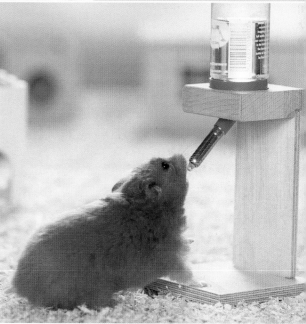

FEEDING PLACE With a dish you have the quantity of food under control to a certain extent. But don't forget that these creatures hoard. Always keep an eye on the entire cage.

Buying a Hamster

The hamster home is ready. But where do you buy a hamster? In addition to pet shops there are at least three other possibilities.

Where Should I Buy My Hamster

The best bet is to buy the animal directly from a professional hamster breeder. That way you not only know the animal's origin, but you also get the most competent advice. Unfortunately, not all breeders sell to private hamster aficionados. So the next best way is to get your new pet from someone you know who already has hamsters and breeds them. If you don't have to have a young animal, you can also inquire if there's a hamster available to a good home in a nearby animal shelter.

If you decide to shop at a pet store, you should put off your visit until the late afternoon hours. The hamsters become active at this time and you can watch all the animals at your leisure. Spend at least

Don't be deceived by little rowdies like these: young hamsters still play with one another. But when they grow older, they will no longer tolerate the presence of other hamsters.

15 minutes doing this. Also ask the age of the animals—they should be four to six weeks old—and compare them with fully grown animals.

Breed and Sex

Surely you have already decided on a Golden or a dwarf hamster. Which breed you now choose is purely a matter of taste, but I always recommend choosing the wild form. Not only do they appear natural, but they also display mostly natural behavior. The sex of the animal (you want to buy and keep just one) is of little consequence; there are hardly any differences in behavior. But for sensitive noses, female hamsters can sometimes have a strong odor. They are ready for mating every four days, and they secrete a small amount of whitish mucus from their sexual orifice, which is the source of this smell. Generally, though, only other hamsters can smell it.

The Way Home

In order to get your new housemate safely home, it's a good idea to buy a travel crate for small animals. This involves an additional purchase, but it makes things pleasant and practical for both the animal and the caregiver. Have the salesperson put a little bedding from the original cage into the crate and carefully put the newly acquired animal in. Half an apple will provide plenty of food and moisture even for a drive of several hours. Never transport your hamster in a car's trunk—the crate will slide around out of control, and (especially in the summer) the temperature is often very high.

Buying a Hamster Made Easy

TIPS FROM
THE HAMSTER EXPERT
Peter Fritzsche

DECIDE Before buying a hamster, decide what species and breeding form you want.

OBSERVE You should observe the hamsters for at least 15 minutes in the pet shop and compare them with one another.

FUR Is it clean and shiny? Unkempt or mangy fur may be a sign of parasites.

ABNORMALITIES Are there any visible deformities? Note irregularities in the incisor teeth. Are they twisted or curved?

CLEANLINESS Are the anus, muzzle, and nose clean? Ask the shop owner to take the animal out of the cage, and preferably hold it in your own hands.

HEALTH Is the animal breathing calmly, evenly, and noiselessly? The eyes must not be crusted or abnormal in any way.

ACTIVITY Does the animal move normally? Do the limbs touch the ground with every stride? Does the hamster put equal pressure on all paws?

Gentle Acclimation

Once you are home, immediately put the new housemate into the prepared cage. When you do, put in all the bedding from the travel cage. The food dish and water bottle should already be full—and now you should leave the animal alone for a while. The main thing it now needs is peace, preferably for a whole week. Of course you will want and need to observe your new charge. But keep at a distance and avoid frightening it with thoughtless movements. Also, during this time, nothing should change in the cage. Simply replenish the food and water as needed. Under no circumstances should you pick up the house or clean it out at this time.

It is extremely interesting to see how the hamster gradually begins to explore its new house. If you have chosen a male Golden Hamster, you may even be able to see it mark its territory. It rubs its flank glands on all projecting objects. Dwarf hamsters don't have flank glands. They use glands in the stomach region to mark their territory—which, unfortunately, is not so easy to see.

Getting Hamsters Used to People

In acclimating hamsters, we always read about taming them. I don't think this term is particularly accurate, however. The animal's will is not broken, nor is its behavior changed. The hamster simply needs to learn to accept the caregiver in its living space and recognize that there is no associated danger. But what's the best way to accomplish this? The main thing is to get the hamster used to your hand, slowly and with calm movements.

❯ Use no perfumed soaps, and rub your hand with a little bedding. Smell is the animal's strongest sense.

❯ Don't offer the hamster any treats through the bars of the cage. Once the hamster comes out of its house unhesitatingly and takes the food from you, you can progress to the next step.

❯ Carefully open the cage and first offer the food inside. Then place it on your hand and wait until the hamster climbs up to get the treat.

❯ Once the hamster has done this a few times, you can try touching it lightly with your fingers. You can

1 A treat like this one on the hand is not to be scorned. And since there evidently is no danger, it's OK to climb up onto it.

2 Once the hamster has grown used to the hand, use the other one to form a protective "cave" around the animal so that it doesn't fall out.

also hold the other hand a little higher to encourage the animal to climb from one hand to the other.

> Once the hamster is used to your hands, you can attempt to lure it out of the cage. The tasty treat method also works with this. With the cage door open, offer food outside the cage and lure the hamster outside. Once again get it acclimated with calm hand movements. Maybe you have even set up a run (see p. 56) and can use your hands as obstacles that the animal can climb.

Note: It's important not to force the animal, but to let everything happen calmly, with patience and persistence.

The Right Way to Pick Up a Hamster

If the hamster is not yet used to your hand, it's best to refrain from picking it up by hand. Research has shown that this causes significant stress for the little rodents. If you want to clean the cage, rub a glass or a large cup with bedding from the cage and let the hamster run inside it.

Once the animal is no longer afraid, you can attempt to pick it up. Slowly and carefully grasp the hamster from the top and the rear by placing both hands around it like a protective cave. Then slide your hands together underneath the hamster and lift it up. Always make sure that it doesn't jump out of your hands and injure itself.

If the cage is small, or if you have to get the animal out from some cranny, you can also grasp it from behind with one hand. Place your thumb and index together behind the front legs and slide the other hand under the animal.

1 The first step is the approach: Make visual contact, speak softly to the hamster, and avoid abrupt movements.

2 Next, hold out a treat to the animal through the bars of the cage. Let the hamster sniff your finger or hand thoroughly.

3 Once the hamster is no longer afraid, open the cage door. Let it sniff your hand thoroughly and climb onto your hand.

How to Make Your Hamster Feel Comfortable

If you have followed all the advice up to this point, there are no further obstacles to a friendship between the little creature and its big caregiver. Here's a summary of the most important ground rules:

Good Idea

 Before buying a hamster, decide which breed and breeding form you want.

 Set up the entire hamster home in advance with bedding, hamster house, things to keep the animal occupied, food dish, and water bottle.

 Choose your favorite animal at leisure; compare several animals.

Get the hamster home as quickly and as gently as possible.

During the first week, leave the new housemate completely alone so that it can adjust.

Better Not

Never purchase a hamster or other animal as a surprise gift.

Hamsters are not cuddly animals, and thus are not a good choice for small children.

Hamsters are confirmed loners; you should never put several animals into one cage.

Hamsters want to rest during the day. Don't disturb their sleep, and put off attempts at acclimation until the evening hours.

During the first three weeks, avoid cleaning up the cage or changing the setup.

Hamsters and Other Pets

Do you already have a pet, and still really want a hamster? The first thing that occurs to me is that this could be a problem. Of course, it depends on what kind of animal (or animals) you already have. Do they move around freely in the house or are they kept in a cage? Sure, fish in an aquarium and Golden Hamsters will get along just fine, since they practically never cross paths. Even with budgies, zebra finches, and other small birds, there is no problem in getting a hamster. The rule that hamsters are loners and want to stay that way under all circumstances also applies to other small mammals. So never put a hamster in with another rodent, whether guinea pig, rabbit, or rat. Sooner or later, the forced association would end up badly for one of them. Of course, you can keep the creatures in separate cages in a room—just make sure that they have no contact with one another when they are out of the cages. The same of course applies to keeping amphibians or reptiles and hamsters: it's OK to be in the same room, but you'll regret it if they ever meet one another.

Communal life with a dog or cat and a hamster is even more difficult. Cats regard hamsters as prey animals (food) because of their innate behavior. The little creature is thus a continual, irresistible stimulation. Even if you think your cat is so gentle, keep it away from the hamster's cage, and preferably out of the room where it's located. Even if the animals have no direct contact, the attention from a cat is always stressful for the rodent. The same applies to dogs on a slightly lesser scale, although they don't react as strongly to hamsters. As long as you are present, you can even try to let the dog into the room where the cage is.

The mere presence of a cat is a source of incredible stress for a hamster, even if it is safe inside its cage. The hamster room should thus be generally off limits to the little hunter.

The Hamster Is Loose—Now What?

Hamsters sometimes break out of the cage when they have the opportunity. Even during unsecured free play, the creatures can slip away. They are quite curious, and you can't counteract or forbid this impulse. It is merely following its inborn behavior in exploring the environment around its burrow. In the wild, hamsters venture as far as a hundred yards/meters from their burrows, so it is pointless to punish them for their escapes. It's better to appreciate your active, clever pet. The most important thing when the hamster gets out is to remain calm and avoid searching frantically through the whole house. If you are sure that the creature is still in the same room, immediately close the door. If you don't know where the escapee is hiding, try to be as quiet as possible so you can hear it better. Once you discover the hiding place, reduce the hamster's field of movement (such as with a barrier constructed of boards or books). Then place a plastic container or a box near the animal. A cardboard tube like the ones used to mail posters is also a good choice.

It's so nice and warm in here. It's also a great hiding place. When your hamster is free, it curiously explores its surroundings.

Now, if you slowly move your hand toward the hamster, there is a good chance that it will flee into the "hole." Now all you have to do is pick the container up and carry the little creature inside it back to its cage.

Looking for a Trail

If you can't find your hamster in spite of a very intensive search, it's a good idea to lure it out of its hiding place with its favorite food. Put a piece of apple, a peanut, a couple of raisins, or even an unaccustomed sweet into the cage and place it onto the floor. If the cage is too large, you can also use the travel cage or a box. In addition to the food, place a little straw from the cage inside and settle down to lie in wait.

A "Hamster Trap" If nothing works, a live trap from the pet shop will help. It is baited with a tempting morsel. When the hamster takes the food, the hinged door closes behind it. Here's a second, equally effective version: put a little straw from the cage into a bucket and put some of your hamster's favorite food in with it. Now all you need to do is to lean a plank up to the bucket or place a stack of books next to it. Then you merely need to wait; it's even best to leave the room. Very rarely can a hamster resist this type of offering. It will climb up to the rim of the bucket and fall in.

If your comrade is really clever, place a cloth over the mouth of the bucket and lay an extra treat onto it. When the hamster tries to get it, it plops down into the bucket along with the cloth.

Now Where Is It Hiding? The treat method also helps when you don't know in which room the hamster is hiding. Put five treats into each room and shut the doors. The next morning you will see where something is missing.

A hamster trap: When the escapee tries to grab the apple, the cloth gives way and down it goes into the bucket.

General Care

In addition to the right accommodations, proper care and nutrition are especially important in keeping your little buddy feeling fine. If you take care of it every day, you will also quickly see when something is wrong or your hamster is sick.

About Wild Animals and House Pets

Knowledge of hamster life in the wild has increased significantly in recent years. Pet owners are taking advantage of this. The more scientists learn about the lifestyle of these little fellows, the better we can meet their requirements.

It's Fun to Hoard

Golden Hamsters, which so far have been studied more than all other species, keep their burrow extremely clean. They even put in an extra room for use as a toilet. There is another room set aside exclusively for food storage—and of course this one should always be as full as possible.

Hoarding Is Vitally Important When winter draws to an end, an intense time begins for the hamster. From the end of winter through June the animals must find enough to eat, give birth to their young, and store up supplies. Only the animals that have gathered enough food can survive the dry summer and the coming winter. So, over time, hoarding has become an important, inborn behavior.

Secure Prey Nowadays, the little mammals prefer to dig their burrows in fields worked by humans. That way, they largely avoid the dangers that normally await them as they search for food: roaming dogs, foxes, snakes, birds of prey, and owls. Sometimes even storks can be observed waiting patiently by a hamster burrow to snap them up at the right moment.

Our house pets don't need to fear any of this—but yet they can't stop hoarding. As a pet owner, you need to keep this in mind, along with your hamster's other preferences, as you provide care and nutrition.

What Your Hamster Likes to Eat

In the wild, hamsters search for their own food. With house pets, this duty falls to you. Food for a hamster consists of three components:
> Dry plant food, which makes up about fifty percent of the food
> Fresh food (around 40 percent)
> Animal protein (10 percent)
Keep this in mind when you choose food, and your little friend will remain healthy and vital for a long time.

Dry Plant Food

Food mixes for small animals provide the majority of their nutrition. You can get this food in pet shops, supermarkets, or some general stores. It consists of various types of grains, oatmeal, sunflower seeds, dried vegetables, dried animal food, and special food flakes (see facing page, photo 5).

What to Look for Even though none of the food mixes are harmful, not every food is really good for hamsters. A glance at the packaging will help you choose; it specifies the composition of the food. Compare various types and choose one that contains as little sugar and fat as possible. The gross fat content should not exceed five percent. In addition, the food should contain 15–20 percent protein.

How Much Food Should I Give? Provide enough food so that your hamster can eat whenever it wants. A good guideline is one to two teaspoonfuls of food mixture per day. Don't be surprised if the food dish is empty again after a short time. Peek into the house or another corner of the cage and you will know why, because your little friend surely has set aside a small supply.

Note: Don't buy too much food at once. The mixture sometimes contains moth eggs. Once the larvae hatch, they will fill up the kitchen in no time.

Dried Plants In order to increase the fiber content of your hamster's food, in addition to the commercially manufactured dry food mix, you can always offer dried plants. Hay is the best option for this (see photo 6). Always make sure that some of this is in the cage; some of it will also be diverted to building a nest. Buy hay with as high a content of meadow herbage as possible. Of course, you can also gather greens yourself and dry them in a shady location. But don't gather the greens from the edge of a busy road or a place where dogs have been walked.

Home Grown

TASTY The following plants are ideal for hamsters: clover, lucerne, dandelion, plantain (all types), daisy, stinging nettle, chamomile, balm-mint, mint, parsley, and other garden herbs, as well as echinacea.

GROWING YOUR OWN If you have a yard or a balcony, you can grow the herbs yourself.

Fresh Food

Wild hamsters don't drink. They meet their need for fluids with fresh foods, which contain lots of water. The rodents also take in lots of vitally important vitamins and minerals with fresh greens. Your little friend needs this even though you regularly provide it with fresh water.

Carrots (careful: don't feed them the tops), apples, and cucumbers constitute fresh food throughout the year. For variety, you can also offer pieces of pear, lettuce (preferably iceberg), soy sprouts, pumpkin, beets, strawberries, and rose hips, depending on the season. You can also offer some of the herbs you dry along with the hay while they are still fresh (see p. 33, photos 2, 3, and 4).

The Right Quantity No matter how healthy it may be, never feed too much green food at one time. It goes bad quickly, and thus is often the cause of intestinal troubles in hamsters. The best course is to offer small quantities of fresh food every day. Before you put it into the cage, check to see if there are any leftovers from the previous day in the cage or the sleeping house. If so, remove them. Over time, you will get a clear idea of how much your charge needs.

A pot of cat grass provides ample variety. Your hamster can climb around in it and eat it. The little Chinese Hamster obviously enjoys it.

Good for the Teeth Hamsters are rodents, so they should always have an opportunity to use their incisors. Put fresh twigs and leaves into the cage (e.g., from apple, pear, beech, or hazelnut trees). Of course, you must make sure that the trees neither grow right next to a road, nor have been sprayed with pesticides.

Protein

In order to supply their protein needs, hamsters in the wild (especially dwarf hamsters) eat not only greens, but also animal food such as insect larvae and grasshoppers. The extra protein plays a major role, especially during pregnancy and nursing of the young. Commercially manufactured food mixes already contain a certain amount of protein. But you should still provide additional nutrition once or twice a week.

Fresh Protein One possibility is to feed small quantities of cottage cheese or other cheese, hamburger, or canned dog food. Simply dip a finger in cottage cheese and hold it out to the hamster. Does it lick your finger clean? Try various things. Like other creatures, hamsters have different taste preferences. But don't feed too much: one fingertip per meal is enough. If you want to use a dish for the food, remove it from the cage the following day.

Live Food If you have no inhibitions, you can even give the hamster live food (available in pet shops). Mealworms are the easiest. Use some tweezers to give your animal one or two of them per week (see photo 1, p. 33). You can also put a living cricket or grasshopper into the cage and watch your hamster hunt.

Caution: **Unhealthy**

DO NOT FEED

SWEETS	May gum up the cheek pouches
RODENT DROPS	Contain too much sugar
SALTED NUTS	The salt damages kidneys
COOKIES	Unless they contain no sugar or salt
CABBAGE	Causes gas
ONIONS AND LEEKS	Cause gas
CERTAIN TYPES OF VEGETABLES	Spinach, beans, sorrel, rhubarb, and raw potatoes are hard to digest
CITRUS FRUITS	Contain too much citric acid
ACIDIC FRUITS	Peaches, apricots, nectarines, pineapple, raspberries, etc., cause excess acidity
HOUSE PLANTS	Potentially poisonous
TWIGS FROM EVERGREEN TREES	Contain undigestible ethereal oils and resins
CERTAIN DECIDUOUS PLANTS	Horse Chestnut, oak, and ivy (also acorns and chestnuts) contain such things as hydrocyanic acids.
EGG YOLK	Contains too much fat (egg white is permissible)
PORK	Likewise too fatty (including ground pork)

A Clean Cage

First the good news: as far as care is concerned, hamsters are not very demanding. They also don't smell as strong as mice or rats whose cage has not been cleaned for some time. It is almost more common to clean the cage too frequently rather than too rarely. A thorough cleaning of the cage, combined with a change of bedding, is necessary only once a month for a hamster that's kept alone. You already know that hamsters are sensitive to changes in their accustomed surroundings, and react to new scents. This includes when you fiddle around in the cage too often.

Even caring for the animal itself is not very demanding, because hamsters have an inborn grooming program and take care of keeping themselves clean.

This Golden Hamster bides its time in a bucket with a little old bedding during the major cage cleaning. This shouldn't take too long.

Cage Care

Of course, animals can't be compared to humans. But would you like it if someone put new carpeting in your house and changed all the furniture around every few days? Then why should a hamster like it? So take it easy with the cage care.

What You Need to Do Every Day Check the food dish every day and fill it when necessary. Leave hoarded seed food right where it is, but remove leftover fresh food from the cage. Even with the daily check into the sleeping house, a deposit of seed food is permissible, but any leftover fresh food must be removed. Also check the water level in the bottle and add water as needed.

Once a Week Is Enough Once a week, take the food dish out of the cage and clean it thoroughly with hot water, but not detergent. The water bottle is also cleaned with a bottlebrush and hot water, then filled up again. Once a week, remove the bedding from the corner that's used as a urinal (see box on facing page).

Once a Month The cage should be cleaned thoroughly every four weeks. During the process, place your hamster with a little bedding from the cage into its travel crate or an empty bucket. Then remove all bedding, along with hoarded food. Take off the bottom tray and clean it with hot water and detergent that doesn't contain much scent. You don't have to use special disinfectants. With stubborn residues simply soften up the affected spot with a little vinegar. Finish up by wiping off the bars of the cage with vinegar and water. Use a brush to dry clean all accessories and the sleeping house. Rinse plastic or ceramic items with hot

Back in the cage at last. If you put everything back in its accustomed place and the hamster recognizes its home by smell, it immediately feels secure again. But a new cage full of strange smells causes lots of stress and really makes its heart race.

water (but no detergent). Once everything is dry, put new bedding into the cage and put everything back where it was. You can also create a familiar environment by putting some old bedding into the cage.

The Urinal Corner

Hamsters generally deposit urine in the same place—usually in a corner of the cage. Look for this spot, and once a week use a small shovel to carefully remove the soiled bedding. Replace it with new shavings.

A Little Primer on Hamster Care

Do you observe your hamster every day? Great! This is the best opportunity to detect any changes, such as soiling of the fur on the legs or around the muzzle and anal region.

An Attractive Coat

Since hamsters regularly groom themselves thoroughly, it's rare for their fur to be dirty—so visible changes usually indicate illness. More on this later.

Observe your charge after it's had its daily rest and is taking care of its "morning toilet" chores. Using both forepaws, or else alternating between left and right, it will clean the area around its snout. Especially with dwarf hamsters, in order to encourage coat care, you should put a small dish of chinchilla sand into the cage. Many (if not all) hamsters will roll in it, which is good for the fur. On the other hand, the little fellows don't have any use for a bath in water. That would also be unhealthy for them.

Long Hair, More Care The longhaired Teddy hamsters require a little more care. Their fur can become matted or stuck together, especially with leftover food. Since the long fur is the result of breeding encouraged by humans, the animals can't groom themselves adequately. Cleaning a mane of this type is simply not part of the hamster's natural grooming program. If you own a longhaired hamster, you must help it from time to time. The anal region of Teddy hamsters is particularly prone to matting. Try to provide some help with a comb or a toothbrush. Always comb or brush gently in the direction of the fur. Despite all your good

intentions, the hamster won't like it, so you will have to hold it securely. If combs and brushes don't help, it's best to trim off the matted hair with scissors. Don't worry: the hair will grow back.

Claw and Tooth Care

In contrast to guinea pigs, hamsters' claws generally don't need to be trimmed. Altering the teeth is also not usual. You can encourage wearing them down by putting twigs or pieces of wood into the cage. Many hamster owners recommend hanging up a piece of limestone or mineral stone. I personally find this unnecessary with adequate variety in the food. And usually the hamsters don't show any interest in the stones.

Avoid **Stress**

THE RIGHT TIME Heart rate measurements have shown clearly how much stress hamsters experience when they are held in the hand or when their cage is changed. Since this stress is particularly high during the day (the hamster's rest time), you should put off all care giving operations and cage cleaning until their active evening hours.

WEIGHING It's easy to check your little friend's health if you weigh it once a week. It's best to use a digital scale and enter the reading into your hamster diary. If the weight changes by a quarter-ounce (7 grams) or more in a week, there is cause for concern. In this case, don't hesitate to call the vet to find out what's wrong with your little friend.

TRIMMING The fur of long-haired Teddy hamsters tends to become matted. If your hamster is used to being held in the hand, trimming the fur is the best and most effective solution. Hold the animal and cut its hair. To avoid hurting the hamster, always hold the scissors parallel to the little body. And don't be sad—the fur will soon grow back in its former beauty.

COMBING If the fur is not too long and matted too tightly, you can also try to comb it out. But for the animal, this procedure is usually less pleasant than trimming.

Is My Hamster Sick?

With proper care, hamsters are not particularly susceptible to disease. There also are no typical hamster diseases. It's equally rare for a sick hamster to infect its owner. Exceptions are fungal infections and the rare LCM (see p. 42).

But how do you determine if your hamster is sick? Of course, the best way is to observe its appearance and behavior regularly. Another important sign for your hamster's health or illness is its body weight, so weigh it regularly—preferably once a week (see also p. 58).

A few typical symptoms of illness are in the box on page 43. If you notice one of these symptoms in your hamster, or are uncertain whether everything is all right, you should definitely consult a vet. You must not try to treat the animal yourself. Time is precious with the little rodents.

Note: On the way to the vet's, consider whether anything has changed recently: did you try out a new food? Did you give more fresh food, or a different type? Was the hamster let out of its cage? Did the temperature in the cage change?

The Most Common Illnesses

The following illnesses are the most common ones that afflict hamsters:

Mites or Fungal Infestation The hamster scratches frequently and is restless. The fur is unkempt in places, or even falls out. If the skin in these places is red or scaly, it indicates a skin fungus. Hold the hamster over a piece of white paper and comb or stroke its fur. With a mite infestation the parasites will fall out; you can see them with a magnifying glass. However, fungi leave no trace behind.

The cause of a parasitic infestation is often rooted in reduced immune system capabilities. This in turn can be caused by improper living conditions such as neglecting to take care of the cage, or inadequate food. But even excessive cleanliness can keep the hamster from building up adequate immunity.

A heat lamp often accelerates healing. But the animal must be able to get out of the heated area.

In any case, you must not experiment with sprays or similar things, but instead get to the vet right away. The vet will not only give you a precise diagnosis, but also clarify in conversation with you what the cause(s) of the sickness may be.

Note: Does your hamster have a fungus? Then always wash and disinfect your hands after holding or petting it.

Lip Scab Fungi and bacteria are also the cause of changes in the muzzle region. They occur mainly through vitamin deficiencies and are aggravated by stress and improper living conditions. You can help your creature recover its health with appropriate salves from the vet and a change in food.

Diarrhea Is your hamster mostly inactive, and is it not eating? Is its anal region soiled? Are the droppings not properly formed, but runny or even watery? Then you need to treat it quickly and visit the vet. If the sickness is acute, the patient can die within 24 hours if you do nothing or the wrong thing. The most important thing is for the hamster to drink. If it doesn't drink on its own, use a plastic syringe without a needle to pour some lukewarm chamomile tea down its throat. Also clean the animal's anal region.

The cause of diarrhea is usually improper or treated fresh food, or an overall change in food. Sometimes, too, a hamster will gnaw on something while it's outside the cage.

Cold The signs of a cold in a hamster are similar to the situation with a human: it sneezes and wheezes as it breathes. The nose runs and the eyes are red. If the animal has been sick for some time it eats less and loses weight. There are many causes for a cold: draft, stress, and improper food may be responsible. In any case, go to the vet, because in some circumstances treatment with antibiotics is advisable. You can also encourage convalescence

1 HOLDING Grasp the hamster this way so you can examine it effectively using a grip that's not too loose or too tight.

2 MEDICATION Use a syringe without a needle to supply the hamster with vitally essential fluid. If necessary, the water can be replaced by medicine.

3 DAMP FUR If the area around the hamster's tail is continually wet, there is cause for concern. Take the hamster to the vet.

with heat treatment. Use a heat lamp to warm up part of the cage. Measure the temperature in the cage under the lamp. It should not exceed 86° F (30° C). And make sure that the hamster has room to get out of the heat.

Wet Tail Disease This illness often afflicts fairly young animals. The hamsters experience a wet area around the tail, usually diarrhea, and weight loss. Here, too, you must immediately seek out a vet. The causes are similar to those for diarrhea. In addition, there is the stress that a young hamster

experiences through separation from the mother or a change in caregiver.

Problems with the Cheek Pouches

If the hamster is given sweets, it is bad for its stomach. In addition, the sugar can gum up the cheek pouches. The animal then keeps trying unsuccessfully to empty them. If you notice this condition, the vet will have to help. Otherwise, the result may be infections and abscesses in the cheek pouches.

Diabetes (Sugar Disease) With improper nutrition, a hamster can also become diabetic. Then, as with many small animals, the cornea of the eye gets cloudy. The animal becomes overweight and the urinal corner is continually wet. Once the vet diagnoses diabetes, it is usually too late. So don't give any sweets.

Hard Spots and Sores Older animals in particular sometimes have bumps on or under the skin. But sores can also occur unseen inside a hamster. If you detect something in feeling the hamster over, sometimes an operation can help.

Further Illnesses Hamsters sometimes suffer broken bones, bite wounds, heat shock, and eye diseases. In all cases visit a vet, who will know the best course of action.

Lymphocytic Choriomeningitis (LCM)

Hamsters can communicate meningitis to humans. Possible symptoms are fever, exhaustion, headaches, and joint and muscle pains. In recent years such infections have become very isolated—

Is the hamster sick? A cloth over the cage will help it rest, and that encourages healing.

and only among people who have had professional contact with rodents. LCM tends to occur in young hamsters that have had contact with infected mice, for example in animal breeding facilities. If you think you are experiencing such symptoms after getting a young hamster, immediately go to your doctor and tell him that you have a hamster.
Note: An infection during pregnancy can lead to

miscarriage. Pregnant women should avoid all contact with hamsters.

Typical **Symptoms** and their **Treatment**

SYMPTOMS, BEHAVIOR	DISEASE	FIRST AID
Inactive, stays in house, doesn't eat, trembles and is fearful, scratches, moves irregularly	All diseases possible Broken bone Heat shock	No stress; shade the cage; with heat shock, cool with damp towels; vet
APPEARANCE Diarrhea, wet rear end, vaginal discharge, bent posture, weight loss or gain, bloated, hard stomach, protruding testes	Intestinal disease, wet tail disease; with vaginal discharge the female may be in estrus; in hot summer weather the testes protrude	Check food, stop giving fresh food, give water; vet; estrus and swollen testes are not a disease
FUR AND SKIN Ruffled, hair loss, sores, injuries	Mite infestation, fungal infestation, tumors, bite wounds	Vet, sprays, and salves
NOSE Sneezing, nasal discharge, noisy breathing	Cold	Correct cause, heat lamp, vet
MOUTH Crusty, saliva discharge, irregular teeth, visible cheek pouches	Fungal and bacterial infestation, dental abnormality, plugged cheek pouches	Vet
EYES Red, crusted, protruding, tears, dry	Keratoconjunctivitis (eye infection)	Vet, salves

Behavioral Peculiarities in Hamsters

Illnesses are not the only things that can spoil the relationship with your pet; its conspicuous behavior patterns can have the same effect. But you can do some things to contribute to your common happiness.

Behavior Stereotypes

When an animal keeps repeating the same action with no apparent purpose for a fairly long time, we can speak of stereotypes. For example, there are hamsters that continually gnaw on the cage bars. Others keep running along the same stretch, usually along one wall of the cage. Still others ceaselessly jump upward in one corner of the cage—a behavior that is particularly common when a hamster is kept in a glass terrarium. The cause of such behavioral stereotypes is inadequate, usually excessively monotonous, living conditions. For you as a responsible hamster owner, this means that you can avoid abnormal behavior by providing the right type of cage and ways for the animal to keep occupied (see p. 50). Once this behavior occurs, it is very difficult or impossible to correct through training. But try, with a new, larger cage, more activity, and more time for running free.

A Shy Hamster

If the hamster scarcely comes out of its cage, there may be a variety of reasons. If the animal is new and still young, there is no cause for alarm. Simply allow the animal a little more time for acclimation, and never force it to do anything. You will achieve trust only by approaching it calmly and carefully. If your hamster previously acted "normally," it may be ill. In this case, check its appearance and weight, and get advice from a vet if necessary. If there are no signs of illness, there remains only the possibility that your hamster is continually stressed out by something. Did you or someone else disturb it during its daytime sleep? Could the condition be treated with the necessary calm? Small children in particular are often impatient and demand too much from the new housemate. Speak with your children and explain to them that the hamster must carefully get used to the caregiver, and especially must not be awakened during its rest time.

Once a hamster gets used to *its* human, it will even eat out of the person's hand.

Hamster Bites

Although hamsters rarely snap, it may happen that your rodent bites you or your child. For example, this may happen if you pick it up carelessly. Perhaps, too, your little companion also wants to see what it's like to bite the new "food" when you stick your finger through the cage bars. This type of bite heals quickly and generally requires no special treatment.

But if the hamster fails to become friendly and keeps trying to bite, it is often due to a lack of patience in getting it acclimated to humans. In this case the only cure is the method involving careful, gradual trust building.

1 GNAWING ON THE CAGE BARS When a hamster continually gnaws on the cage bars, we speak of a behavioral stereotype. Usually a lack of ways to keep occupied is responsible for the unusual behavior. The most effective way to avoid this abnormality is through a variety of cage accessories and frequent opportunities to get exercise outside the cage.

2 BEWARE OF THE HAMSTER Does your hamster fail to get used to humans? Does it try to bite every time someone tries to get close? Maybe it has had bad experiences with humans, was awakened often during its sleep phase, or stressed in other ways. There's only one cure for this: lots of patience and a gradual process of getting used to one another—step by step.

3 VERY SHY Whereas many hamsters bite (see photo 2), others seek salvation in flight and are especially shy. The animals stay behind their hamster houses and come out only for a short time to gather food. This behavior comes from a fear of the caregivers and their hands. The only solution is to build trust slowly and carefully.

Hamster Reproduction

This book is not intended as a guide to raising hamsters. Breeding these cute rodents should be reserved for professional hamster breeders. They know precisely when and which animals to mate and can provide the best conditions for raising the young. Also, with professionals there are regulations governing adoption or sale of young animals. Nevertheless, lay people often experience reproduction of their hamsters, too. Oftentimes a male and a female of one litter are kept together in a cage. If the animals are not sold immediately, it may happen that they have already mated when

they come into your possession. If you have bought a female, one day you may hear a peeping and squeaking from the hamster house.

Mating Behavior

Golden Hamsters living in the wild leave their burrows in March, after their winter sleep. After they have eaten, the males go looking for a partner. They keep checking the female's burrow in the evening to see if the lady hamsters want to mate with them. The females are ready to mate every four days. When a male meets a willing female, she mates with him; several egg cells in the female's body are fertilized. Hamster love doesn't last long; immediately after pairing, the males and females part company. Golden Hamster females then act very aggressively toward males and want to have nothing to do with them. So professional breeders separate the sexes immediately after mating, or they keep the hamsters in such large cages that the males can hide.

Gestation and Birth

Of all mammals, hamsters have the shortest gestation period. With Golden Hamsters, it takes just 16 days for the young to see the light of day. With the Phodopus Dwarf Hamsters, the gestation period is only two days longer; with the Chinese Hamster pregnancy lasts 20 days in all. During this

A nest with seven-day-old Golden Hamsters. Their fur is already starting to grow, so the mother can leave them alone for a longer time.

1 NICE AND WARM These Djungarian Dwarf Hamsters are already quite developed and can control their body temperature themselves.

2 A RUNAWAY The young ones are curious. But usually their journeys of discovery are restrained by the mother, who carries them back to the nest. Father hamsters don't do this.

3 SAYING GOOD-BYE Once the young can eat independently, they are separated from the mother. But siblings can stay together.

time the expectant mother diligently collects nest material and prepares the birthing nest. Cellulose in particular is gratefully accepted for cushioning. At the same time, the female takes in lots of high-protein nutrients. In addition to the usual amount, breeders now feed cottage cheese, fresh cheese, and insects.

The Babies Are Born When the time is right, a female brings one youngster after another into the world, usually in the early morning hours. With Golden Hamsters, there is an average of eight young, and the record is 17. Campbell's and Djungarian Dwarf hamsters give birth to about six young, and the other two species often produce fewer. The entire birthing process lasts around an hour. Immediately thereafter, the mother licks the young clean, and they begin to suckle.

While giving birth, the female hamster reacts particularly sensitively to disturbances. If she believes that the young are in danger, she may even start to eat them. This behavior is termed kronismus by biologists, and it is not really a behavior abnormality but rather a completely

natural defensive mechanism. Raising the young requires lots of energy on the part of the mother. All her strength would be wasted if the young fell victim to enemies. For this reason, it is better for continued survival to kill the litter in the face of danger. Then the female can quickly produce more young, which will then grow up in a peaceful environment.

A Female Thing With Golden Hamsters, the female is the only one responsible for giving birth and raising the young. The dwarf hamsters are the only ones that tolerate the presence of the male. Many male dwarf hamsters even help to raise the young—for example, by keeping them warm if the mother leaves the nest. According to recent studies by our institute, this is especially the case with Roborovskii's Dwarf Hamsters. The males of Campbell's Dwarf Hamsters and Chinese Hamsters, on the other hand, play a much smaller role in caring for the young.

Hamster Development

Young hamsters stay in the nest for a long time. At birth they are naked, blind, and completely helpless. Newborn hamsters weigh just a fraction of an ounce (two grams). Their skin is reddish to pink, and the little ones would freeze if they weren't warmed by the mother (or the father, in the case of dwarf hamsters). But as soon as the fourth day of life, the young have not only doubled in weight, but also begin to grow lots of fur. At first, Golden Hamsters appear to be gray, but the first light brown hair becomes visible starting on the fifth day. From this point on, their sense of smell is so highly developed that they can recognize their own nest. The young animals probably can also hear at this point. If they feel abandoned, they emit ultrasound calls, as bats do, that are perceptible to the mother, but not to enemies. On the sixth day, the hamsters begin to crawl, but it takes another whole week for their eyes to open.

For three months, the female supplies the offspring

This Golden Hamster is already more than two years old. Its fur has become thinner and it has lost weight. An old animal needs lots of rest, but still enjoys getting spoiled with a treat.

with milk. Then the youngsters are able to find food for themselves. From this point on, part of the routine involves excursions to the hamster burrow. We now know that the mothers leave their young after four weeks. They are still tolerated in the burrow for a while, where she can protect them from enemies that lie in wait for them outside. After that they have to take care of themselves and start their own families. And that happens quickly—the young are sexually mature after just 40 days and can beget and give birth to young.

Old Hamsters

At the start of this book, I mentioned that hamsters don't live to be old. In the wild, an animal that was born in April or May probably dies as early as the fall of the following year. A well–cared–for pet that gets proper nutrition and good care can live to the age of two to three, and often even four. The following signs show that your friend is getting old:
> In the evening it no longer comes out of its sleeping house right away, but instead often stays inside for a long time.
> It uses its exercise wheel less frequently.
> The fur becomes unkempt, and the animal even loses hair.
> The animal eats less and visibly grows thinner.

A Gentle Goodbye

Let your hamster enjoy the evening of its life in comfort and peace. Pamper it with some of its favorite treats. Give it lots of rest. It may not need to get out and run around any more. One day you will find it rolled up and lifeless in its sleeping house. It has died.

Advice for Parents

TIPS FROM THE
HAMSTER PRO
Peter Fritzsche

PREPARATION Have a timely conversation with your child and explain why the hamster won't live much longer. Tell the child that the hamster has had it good, but that hamsters live only a short time. Perhaps your child will understand that animals and plants have to die so that life on earth can exist.

FAREWELL Children get over the pain of loss more effectively when they can bury their dead animal in the yard or some other secluded place. Maybe your child will want to put some object that it liked into the grave, such as a handful of hay or some small item from the cage.

SYMPATHY Explain to your child that it is often better for the vet to put a sick animal to sleep to release it from suffering.

SUCCESSION Don't immediately buy a new hamster to comfort the child. Talk about a good time to get another hamster instead.

Staying Active

In the wild, hamsters are very active and sometimes travel for great distances. In so doing, the animals must overcome various obstacles. If you want to keep your friend in the right conditions, you also have to provide variety at home.

How Lively Are Hamsters?

Research is still in its infancy, but it has produced a few results. For example, we have two possibilities for observing nocturnal hamster life. With one method, a small radio-sending unit is attached around the rodent's neck. The attendant receiver picks up the signals from the sender, regardless of whether the hamster is in the burrow or on the surface. A second method was developed in recent years in our institute in Halle, Germany. Plastic rings are placed on the opening of the hamster burrow; they are large enough for the hamsters to pass through comfortably. In each ring there are a small antenna and two photoelectric barriers built in. Then the hamsters are caught, and a small sending unit is implanted under their skin. Since it is as small as a grain of rice, they don't feel it, and it doesn't restrict their movement. As soon as a "chipped" hamster leaves its burrow or returns to it, the movement is captured by the antennas and the photoelectric barriers. An integrated storage system notes all these dates, much like a memory card in a digital camera. Then the researchers can use a computer to evaluate the numbers every couple of days. That way, they find out on what day and at what time which hamster visited which burrow and how long it stayed inside. So, for example, we now know that male hamsters travel great distances, but they visit the females' burrow for only a short time. It is also new knowledge that at night Golden Hamsters stay in their burrow. All of this is important information if you keep a hamster as a pet and want to keep it appropriately occupied.

How Can I Keep My Hamster Occupied?

In pet shops you can get a whole array of more or less appropriate accessories for a hamster cage. In some cases these devices are also called hamster toys. But this is nonsense, for hamsters don't play. They simply explore their surroundings for edibles and appropriate materials for building their nest. Cage accessories stimulate this exploratory urge so that your hamster gets more exercise and has new experiences.

Houses with several stories, small ladders, or seesaws accommodate the hamster's need for climbing; in the wild they can climb out of their burrows with lightning speed. Further good choices are objects with hollows or openings through which the animals can crawl. For a Golden Hamster, this type of opening should be no smaller than 1 3/4 inch (4.5 cm) so that the creature doesn't get stuck. For dwarf hamsters, 1 1/2 inch (4 cm) is adequate.

Homemade Cage Accessories

Even if you are only moderately talented at working with your hands, you can make accessories for your hamster. On the one hand, you rarely find the right items in pet shops. On the other, you can make sure that there are no toxic materials or sharp nails that stand in the way of your little friend's enjoyment.

In theory, everything that will neither harm nor endanger the hamster is appropriate for making accessories. Items made from untreated wood, from printing-free cardboard, from clay, sisal, or non-toxic modeling clay are preferable to all others.

Wood Of course, wood is the first choice among building materials. At the lumberyard, ask for scrap pieces of pine or spruce boards about 3/4 inch (15–20 mm) thick. You can often get these pieces for free. But you must use only wood that has not been treated. Any wood that has been veneered or coated on one side is inappropriate for your needs. But you can consider chipboard as an alternative to real wood. Now all you need is a fine-tooth saw and you can get started. Anyone can make a couple of building blocks that can be stacked up to form different climbing towers (see photo 3 at the right). Or how about a homemade hamster house? This type of hideout should have dimensions of about 8 × 4 inches (20 × 10 cm). You will need four sidewalls four inches (10 cm) high and an appropriate board for the flat roof. The easiest way is to use a coping saw, which you can get inexpensively in any hardware store.

Hold the pieces together with wood glue or wooden dowels. If you varnish the house it will last longer and be easier to clean. But use only special varnish that is suitable also for children's toys (also

Caution: **Danger**
SAFETY: With accessories, make sure there are no sharp nails or screws sticking out that could injure the animals. Since hamsters are rodents and may destroy an object over time, nails and such must not be exposed through repeated gnawing. The best choice for holding things together: glue or wooden dowels.

available in building supply stores).

Once you have mastered your first item in style, you may attempt other devices and create such things as a bridge or a seesaw for the little fellow (see p. 53, photos 2 and 5).

Clay and Other Materials Clay is almost easier to work than wood. You can form good caves and bowls from the white or brown mass that you can buy at any good crafts store. You can cure the finished products in an oven at 485° F (250° C) or simply let them air dry. Further appropriate materials for hamster accessories include *papier mâché* made from newspaper and wallpaper paste (e.g., in several layers applied over a balloon),

sturdy cardboard (preferably with no printing on it), and foam mortar (from a building supply store).

Exercise Wheel

What first pops into your mind when you think of accessories for the hamster cage? Probably the exercise wheel (see p. 53, photo 1). There is a lot of discussion about the pros and cons of this device. Some feel that the wheel is a good way to combat boredom, but others maintain that it's an addiction for the hamster. Scientific research has shed some light on the use of the exercise wheel. I personally was involved in research in which hamsters that lived both with and without an exercise wheel were compared. The results were clear, and I can recommend that every hamster owner equip the cage with an exercise wheel. Hamsters that run have fewer behavior problems, build more muscle, are healthier, and have more offspring than their counterparts that live in a cage with no exercise wheel. But there is one limitation: not all exercise wheels are the same. The devices must satisfy a couple of requirements. For example, they must have at least a 10-inch (25-cm) diameter for Golden Hamsters, and at least an eight-inch (20-cm) diameter for dwarf hamsters.

The width of the enclosed running surface should be about three inches (8 cm). In addition, one side of the exercise wheel should be closed. But metal or spoked exercise wheels are less appropriate. The hamster can easily get caught in them and injure itself.

This type of house is great for climbing and exploring. At the same time, the little rodent can use its teeth on the wood.

1 A TUNNEL SYSTEM This type of construction made from wooden tubes is similar to the passageways in the burrow of hamsters living in the wild.

2 MAINTENANCE If the tubes are not too long and are adequately ventilated with openings, the hamster will take to the system and explore it with lots of interest.

3 APPROPRIATE A variety of exercise improves your charge's well-being and prevents behavior stereotypes.

A System of Tubes

With accessories similar to tubes you can accommodate the hamster's natural behavior very well. For example, you can simply connect the hamster house with a second house that serves as a food warehouse. It's even better to connect two cages using tubes. The recommended diameter for the passageways is around 1 3/4 inches (4.5 cm). Also, the tubes should be no longer than a foot (30 cm). It can't be helped if your hamster sometimes uses the tunnel as a toilet. So from time to time the tube will need to be cleaned. Just as important as the proper dimensions is adequate ventilation, so it makes sense to drill holes into the tubes. But they must be small enough so that the hamster can't get its feet caught in them. If you don't have the patience to do this yourself, get some flexible drainage pipe (from a hardware store) that already has holes in it.

Note: I don't recommend the colorful, ready-made tube systems from pet shops. Aside from the price, they are inappropriate for a hamster for a number of reasons. For example, oftentimes they don't have enough ventilation. In addition, many types collect so much urine that the result is a high concentration of ammonia.

Sand Bath

Dwarf hamsters really enjoy having a sand bath. They clean their fur in it and, in the wild, they use it to get rid of annoying parasites (see p. 53, photo 4). Get some chinchilla sand from a pet shop and put it into a shallow ceramic dish that you place inside the cage.

Free Exercise—A Change from the Cage Routine

The most interesting change of pace for a hamster involves getting out of the cage and exploring new territory. It's also pleasant for you to watch it in action.

Out of the Cage

First of all, the most important point: in contrast to rabbits and guinea pigs, unfortunately there can be no running free in the yard or on the balcony for hamsters. There simply are too many dangers for these little animals. In addition, hamsters are quite clever, and your friend would surely find an opportunity to disappear, never to be seen again. Thus, the free exercise should take place only indoors, and preferably in a course set up for the purpose. The hamster should be able to get to it through the open cage door without your help. A small ramp or a ladder can be helpful, and at the same time it constitutes the first challenge for the climbing wizard.

A hamster can't get enough free exercise. When the "pen" is secure, the hamster can move around and keep busy inside it. A blanket or a piece of carpet keeps the floor clean.

Security Measures To make sure that nothing happens to your hamster, you must take a few precautionary measures. The hamster must not come into contact with any of the following items: poisonous houseplants, anything with an electrical current (such as wall sockets and electrical cords), lighted candles, heating elements, sharp or pointed objects, and other pets. Because of the danger of slipping, it is also undesirable for a hamster to run on smooth surfaces such as tiles, laminate, parquet, or linoleum. Carpeted floors are good, however. In addition you must be sure that your charge has no opportunity to get away and disappear in cracks or spaces under pieces of furniture, in vases, or out an open window. So tighten everything down. You can play it safe by closing in the free exercise area with a few 12-inch boards or heavy cardboard strips.

Exercise Equipment

In contrast to the restrictions of the cage, you have a lot more room to work with in setting up the exercise area. You can set up a system of tunnels using scraps of wood and branches, which the hamster can explore. Or you can construct a maze from wood or stones. You will be amazed how quickly your animal will learn to master this. Put in a fairly large container of sand or loose garden peat in which the hamster can dig at will. Sow some wheat seeds or grass seeds in a shallow dish with a little dirt or cellulose. When the plants are fairly large, give the dish to the hamster to explore and eat. On the topic of eating, you can hide little pieces of food in the exercise enclosure. That will whet your friend's curiosity even more.

Exercise with a Fun Factor

TIPS FROM THE
HAMSTER EXPERT
Peter Fritzsche

CLEAN There's no way to keep a hamster from depositing droppings or urine when it's exercising. If you are concerned that the carpet will become soiled, simply spread out an old sheet on the location for the exercise area. At the end you can easily roll it up and wash it from time to time.

SAFE If the hamster runs free around the room, you must first secure all the furniture under which it could crawl. You can simply put down some foot-high (30-cm) boards or strips of cardboard or plastic. You can also use these to prevent contact with dangerous items such as poisonous house plants, wall sockets, and electrical cables. A strip in front of the door will keep your hamster from making a break for it if you have to leave the room for a moment.

UNDER WATCH The most important thing with all activities outside the cage: never let your hamster out of your view. But if it still manages to slip away, use the tips on page 28 to recapture it.

Suggestions for Hamster Watching

In the following paragraphs I will give you a few tips on how to get to know your hamster better. With this method, you are nearly on your way to becoming a hamster researcher.

Weighing

By weighing your animal regularly (once a week) you get relatively objective information about the overall condition of your animal. The best thing to use is a common kitchen scale with a digital readout. Let the hamster run into a container that it can't get out of too quickly and place it onto the scale. Write down the hamster's weight. Don't forget to subtract the weight of the container from the overall weight. If you have a computer you can even draw a graph that clearly shows the weight changes. If your hamster ever gets sick, you can not only give the vet a printout of the data, but also provide valuable background information.

Daytime Activity

Does your hamster have an established daytime

A hamster is not a cuddly animal. Still, it's lots of fun to watch attentively. That's a good way to discover some interesting behaviors.

schedule? Does its activity change according to the season? Try as often as possible to enter into a chart the times that your animal is awake. A computer graphic can also make any changes stand out—for example, in comparing the warm summer and the cold winter months.

Aptitude for Learning

How intelligent is your charge? Measure how quickly it copes with unaccustomed challenges. For example, have it run through a newly constructed maze during an exercise period (you can find suggestions on how to make one on the Internet). At the end, the hamster gets a little treat. Time how long it takes your hamster and write down its mistakes. How many runs does it take for the time to level off? Another possibility is to train the hamster on shapes (behavior researchers call this "conditioning"). In front of the hamster, place a cardboard box with two openings that you have marked with various symbols in advance (e.g., a cross and a triangle). The spaces behind the two openings must not be connected. Put some of your pet's favorite food behind one of the openings. Now keep changing the position of the box, but always place the food behind the same opening (e.g., the one with the cross). Does the hamster learn to choose the right opening on its own?

Grooming Sequence

Watch precisely how your hamster grooms itself. What movements does it use? Does it use both front paws? How does it use its hind legs? Once you know how it grooms itself, write down the procedure. The grooming sequence is genetically programmed. A behavior researcher can tell by tiny changes whether or not the animal is feeling fine. **Note** Please make sure that your interest in the hamster doesn't turn into a source of stress for it.

Enough running! If your hamster uses its exercise wheel enthusiastically, it's a sign of good health.

Page numbers in **bold type** refer to illustrations.

Clubs and Associations

> Internet Hamster Association of North America
http://groups.msn.com/ InternetHamsterAssoc
"A networking and resource site for hamster enthusiasts."
> Hamster Club of Ontario
http://www.geocities.com/hamster clubofontario/home.html
Members can receive a newsletter four times per year, attend meetings, participate in hamster shows, obtain informational pamphlets, and meet other hamster owners.
> California Hamster Association
http://www.geocities.com/ CalHamAssoc/
A non-profit hamster club in

Southern California interested in educating hamster owners and improving the quality of hamsters in California and North America; arranges competitive hamster shows.
> The National Hamster Council
http://www.hamsters-uk.org
The oldest hamster club in the world. Although it is British, many North American hamster owners join one of its affiliated clubs because there are not many clubs in North America. Information about shows and breed standards is provided.

Hamsters Online

On these Internet sites you can find tips on the feeding, care, and health of hamsters, plus addresses of breeders and clubs:
> *www.petwebsite.com/ hamsters.asp*
> *www.ahc.umn.edu/rar/ MNAALAS/Hamsters.html*
> *http://exoticpets.about.com/ cs.hamsters/a/hamstercare.htm*
> *http://www.hamsterific.com/ SyrianHamsters.cfm*
> *http://www.ask-the-vet.com/ hamster-care.htm*
> *http://www.hamsterhideout. com/allabthams.html*
> *http://www.myhammie.com*
http://www.hookedonhamsters. com
> *http://www.hamster-heaven. com/index.html*

> *http://www.hamsterific. com/DwarfHamsters.cfm*
> *http://russiandwarfhamsters. tripod.com/hams.id1.html*

Helpful Books

> Bartlett, Patricia. *The Hamster Handbook.* Barron's Educational Series, Inc.
> Bucsis, Gerry, and Barbara Somerville. *Training Your Pet Hamster.* Barron's Educational Series, Inc.
> Fritzsche, Peter. *My Hamster.* Barron's Educational Series, Inc.
> Hill, Lorraine. *Hamsters A to Z.* TFH Publications.

Periodical

> *Critters USA* (annual)
AFRMA
9230 64th Street
Riverside, CA 92509-5924

Important Notes

> Sick hamster If your hamster displays symptoms of disease, it belongs under the care of a vet.

> Danger of infection Only a few diseases are communicable to humans. Advise your doctor of your contact with animals. This is especially important if you have been bitten.

> Allergy to animal hair Many people are allergic to animal hair. If you have any doubts, ask your doctor before you buy a hamster.

G|U

The title of the German book is *Hamster*.

English translation by Eric A. Bye, M.A.

All inquires should be addressed to:
Barron's Educational Series, Inc.
250 Wireless Boulevard
Hauppauge, NY 11788
www.barronseduc.com

ISBN-13: 978-0-7641-3927-7
ISBN-10: 0-7641-3927-4

Library of Congress Control No.: 2007041589

Library of Congress Cataloging-in-Publication Data

Fritzsche, Peter.
  [Hamster. English]
  Hamsters : everything about selection, care, nutrition, and behavior / Peter Fritzsche : filled with full-color photographs by Oliver Giel.
    p. cm.
  Includes index.
  ISBN-13: 978-0-7641-3927-7 (alk. paper)
  ISBN-10: 0-7641-3927-4 (alk. paper)
  1. Hamsters as pets.   I. Title.

SF459.H3F74513 2008
636.935'6—dc22

2007041589

Printed in China
9 8 7 6 5 4

The Author

Dr. Peter Fritzsche holds a Ph.D. in Biology and is a scientist at the Institute for Zoology at Martin Luther University in Halle-Wittenberg, Germany. He has researched the behavior of hamsters for around 30 years and is world–renowned as a hamster expert.

The Photographer

Oliver Giel specializes in nature and animal photography and, with his partner Eva Scherer, he handles photo production for books, periodicals, calendars, and advertising. You can find out more about his photo studio at www.tierfotograf.com.
All photos in this book are from Oliver Giel, except for: Peter Fritzsche: p. 6, 8, 10 (bottom two), 19 (left), 48; Regina Kuhn: front cover photo

SOS – What to Do?

Gnawing on the Cage Bars

LONG–TERM: If your hamster continually gnaws on the cage, it probably doesn't have enough to keep it occupied. Perhaps the cage is too small or doesn't have enough accessories. Maybe the hamster doesn't get out of the cage enough. A large exercise wheel will help prevent boredom.

Diarrhea

RIGHT AWAY: Remove all fresh food and fill the water bottle with fresh water. In addition, take the hamster to the vet immediately. It's best if you can also take along a stool sample. Clean the cage and change the bedding. LONG–TERM: Consider changing the food.

Unexpected Offspring

LONG–TERM: Evidently you have selected a female that had previous contact with a male. Just keep calm. The mother will raise the young ones by herself. Stay away from the cage as much as possible. Provide food high in protein and make sure the drinking water is fresh.

Escape

RIGHT AWAY: If you know where the little fellow has crept off to, try to lure it out with its favorite food. Place a dark container (like a cardboard tube or a box) near it and see what happens. LONG–TERM: Always keep the cage closed securely and install boards or cardboard strips to make a high barrier around the free exercise area. If you keep your hamster in an aquarium, you must make sure that it can't climb out by using the exercise wheel. Keep the axle of the wheel lubricated with cooking oil so that it turns when it's touched and can't serve as a ladder.

Biting

RIGHT AWAY: Did you disturb the animal while it was resting? Or is the cage in a noisy location? This is a source of stress, and the hamster is defending itself. LONG–TERM: If your friend is not yet accustomed to people, you need to exercise more patience (see p. 24) and approach it carefully.